MOM,
more than
a *little*

I more than a little *appreciate* you,

and the person you are,

and the things that you do.

There's so much to say,
I don't know where to start...
but then, I remember:
begin with the *heart*.

Because *that* is exactly how you choose to live,
and I don't think you know how uncommon that is.

And the thing that's most clear
when I pause and look back
is the *love* that you brought
to each errand and task...

From phone calls to favors,
late nights to long days,
it's been there since the start,
every bit of the way.

You made everyday moments feel *special* and sweet
with traditions and laughter and favorite treats.

You've shaped my world, made it more beautiful too—
and the years have a glow where your spirit *shines* through.

I'm so grateful for every day you were there
with your presence, your purpose,
your kindness, your *care*.

And although I might not have known it at the time, you set aside *your needs* to focus on *mine*.

When I think of the things that I've done and achieved,
there are many I tried just because you *believed*.

There are lessons you taught me
that *still* shape my days
in all kinds of vast
and remarkable ways...

Like how much one person is capable of
when they live with the right blend
of *hard work* and *love*.

The example you set just by being yourself
has mattered to me more than *anything* else.

I'm more than a little bit grateful, it's true,

for the good things I've learned

just because you are *you*.

I'm writing these words to you,
straight from my heart:
Mom, thank you for everything
that you are.

COMPENDIUM.

live inspired

Written by: M.H. Clark

Illustrated by: Cécile Metzger

Edited by: Amelia Riedler

Art Direction by: Chelsea Bianchini

ISBN: 978-1-957891-07-1

1st printing. Printed in China with soy inks on FSC®-Mix certified paper.

Create meaningful moments with gifts that inspire.

CONNECT WITH US

live-inspired.com | sayhello@compendiuminc.com

@compendiumliveinspired
#compendiumliveinspired